THE IDEOLOGY
OF SAMENESS

THE IDEOLOGY OF

SAMENESS

ALAIN DE BENOIST

ARKTOS
LONDON 2022

Qu'est-ce que l'idéologie du même? published by La Nouvelle Librairie éditions in 2022.

The series *Foundations* is the result of a cooperation between Arktos Media and the Institut Iliade (Paris). The French original is published in the series 'Collection Longue Mémoire de l'Institut Iliade'.

ISBN	978-1-915755-08-7 (Paperback)
	978-1-915755-09-4 (Ebook)
TRANSLATION	Roger Adwan
EDITING	Constantin von Hoffmeister
COVER & LAYOUT	Tor Westman

🌐 Arktos.com   ❦ fb.com/Arktos   ✈ @arktosmedia   ⓞ arktosmedia

CONTENTS

WHAT IS THE IDEOLOGY OF SAMENESS?

B ACK IN 1977, I published a large book entitled *View from the Right*,[1] which was awarded first prize at the essai de l'Académie française a year later and has since been repeatedly reprinted. One of the most frequently quoted sentences of the book's introduction was the following:

> I hereby define the Right, by pure convention, as the consistent attitude to view the diversity of the world, and by consequence the relative inequalities that are necessarily the product of this, as a positive thing; and the progressive homogenisation of the world, extolled and effected by two thousand years of egalitarian ideology, as a negative thing.

At the time, this sentence summarised my way of seeing things most accurately, and even today, I still identify with it to a large extent. Combining the complementary yet distinct notions of diversity and inequality, of homogenisation and equality, this 'anti-egalitarian' profession of faith was, however, rather ambiguous as well. By defining one's struggle against egalitarianism as one's main objective, one obviously ran the risk of appearing to legitimise both various practices

---

1   TN: Published in three volumes by Arktos Media Ltd.

of exclusion (in the name of the purported inferiority of one group or another) and certain liberal elitist methods, with the inequality in people's living conditions seen as a just result of their inherent inequalities, and social justice as a 'pipe dream'. Delving into this complex issue is thus definitely worthwhile.

The Trials and Tribulations of Equality

Equality between A and B (A = B) implies that A is similar or identical to B, thus not differing from the latter, or, alternatively, that they are equivalent to one another in accordance with a specific criterion and as part of a particular relation. One must thus either specify this criterion or identify the relation in question. Julien Freund[2] writes:

> If people or things are only equal under certain conditions, they can still be different or unequal in other respects.[3]

One can thus conclude that equality is never an absolute fact and does not designate any specific relation, depending instead on a certain convention — which, in this case, is either the adopted criterion or the chosen relation. Formulated as a self-sufficient principle, it is devoid of content, for there is no equality or inequality except in a given context and in relation to factors that allow it to be set or assessed in concrete terms. The notions of equality and inequality are therefore always relative and, by definition, never free of arbitrariness.

What is significant here is that we commonly contrast the plural term 'inequalities' with the singular 'equality'. Through the unicity of the very concept, the notion of equality strives, of itself, towards the homogeneous, i.e. towards the unique. This conceptual unity, however, is not echoed by the nature of the empirical forms that it actually

---

2   TN: Julien Freund (8 January 1921–10 September 1993) was a French philosopher and sociologist.

3   AN: Julien Freund, 'Pluralité des égalités et équité' (The Plurality of Equalities and Fair-mindedness), in *Politique et impolitique* (Politics and Impolitics), Sirey, Paris, 1987, page 180.

evokes. The various forms of equality themselves are thus not equal to one another. Insofar as one grants it an absolute sort of value, the notion of equality becomes even more contradictory. No unique value could ever exist, because a value is only determined when compared to others that are worthless (or worth less). Ascribing value to something thus necessarily implies prioritising it, which one does each and every time one establishes equality as one's supreme value. By hierarchising, in fact, one already violates the very principle of equality, a principle that negates any notion of hierarchy (which is equivalent to the contradiction that pacifists find themselves in whenever they are forced to fight against those who do not share their point of view). 'Egalitarianism', adds Julien Freund, 'denies on a theoretical level the very hierarchy that it implies on a practical one. Indeed, it grants superiority and exclusive value to equality in all its forms, thus demoting all relations that are not equal to the rank of lower values ... Therefore, it assesses reality in accordance with an order that contrasts the lower with the higher — in other words, it pragmatically adds to its concept a hierarchy that it theoretically claims to deny and condemn.'[4]

When it strives to establish equivalence, the very notion of value is ambiguous. Indeed, whenever we state that two things are equal, we are not actually claiming that they are one and the same, but rather that they are equal in terms of value despite all that sets them apart. However, the mere fact of emphasising all that makes them similar, no matter how dissimilar they may otherwise be, causes their dissimilarity to recede into the background. Two things that 'are equal' to each other are equal in terms of value. It is thus all too easy to conclude that since they are both defined by what they are worth, they are actually one and the same.

In contrast with proportional equality, mathematical or algebraic equality thus bears within itself a principle of non-differentiation. When applied to human beings, it signifies that there is no difference

---

4   AN: Ibid., page 183.

between them that could be perceived as one to relativise the aspects through which they do not differ. Understood in such a manner, equality results in the removal of anything incommensurable that actually defines the human subject in question. However, abstract equality is also a fundamentally economic notion, because it is only in the economic domain, in relation to the universal equivalent embodied by money, that it can be established, measured and verified. Economics is, alongside moral philosophy (though for other reasons), the primary field in which equality can be assessed, because its accounting unit, namely the monetary one, is interchangeable by definition. Indeed, any dollar or euro is worth another. Only the amount varies; only the quantity specifies. Political or legal equality is, by contrast, an entirely different matter. As for any equality that is neither economic nor political or legal, it is not subject to any specific definition. Any doctrine that claims to adhere to such a notion thus belongs to the sphere of metaphysics.

In the age of modernity, emancipation has long been associated with the desire for equality rather than freedom. With inequality presented as an a priori oppressive structure (which it has admittedly often been), freedom was, in some way, doomed to deny itself insofar as, by allowing or even exacerbating inequalities, it resulted in the re-creation of oppression — so much so that some authors, including Norberto Bobbio, have been led to regard the ideal of equality as the essential agent behind the Right-Left divide. 'The partisan of equality', he writes, 'generally thinks that most inequalities that shock him and that he would like to eradicate are of social origin and can, as a result, be stamped out, whereas, on the contrary, the supporter of inequality believes that, generally speaking, these inequalities are natural and therefore inevitable.'[5]

Is this still true today? Well, it seems to me that in the eyes of the public, taking everyone's tendencies into account, people are now

---

5   AN: Norberto Bobbio, *Destra e sinistra. Ragioni e significati di una distinzione politica*, Donzelli, Roma, 1994.

more aware of the fact that fostering conditions of equality is not necessarily possible, nor even automatically desirable, for that matter. We are less and less inclined to believe that all inequalities are of social origin. Conversely, one can very easily feel that excessive inequalities in terms of income are politically and socially unbearable, without, however, believing in the natural equality of individuals. (It is, moreover, a commonplace of classical thought to assert that excessive wealth erodes virtue.) We also realise that the massification and cultural standardisation conducted in the name of equality (and under the guise of 'democratisation') have more often served the interests of large commercial companies than the ideals of democracy. People strive for equal opportunities more often than for equal results. They tend to differentiate between just and unjust inequalities, between those that are tolerable and those that are not, which amounts to acknowledging that inequality itself, just like equality, has lost all meaning.

Emphasis is now placed on equity rather than on equality, which does not imply the fact of giving everyone the same thing, but of ensuring that everyone gets as much of their due as possible. Instead of aspiring to equality itself, the Left seeks the sustainable maximisation of the minimum (*maximin*) even in economic matters, meaning that it strives for a distribution or redistribution that would bestow as much as possible on those who possess the least, while taking into account, even in their own interest, the positive effect that certain economic disparities could indeed have on inciting people to invest or save. John Rawls[6] was one of the first to systematically present — though admittedly from an essentially procedural point of view — a theoretical foundation for the subordination of the requirement of equality to that of equity.[7] 'Equity', says Julien Freund, 'is the form of justice that initially accepts the plurality of human activities, of people's ambitions

---

6   TN: An American philosopher.

7   AN: John Rawls, *A Theory of Justice*.

and aspirations, of their interests and ideas, and endeavours to proceed by way of compensation in the unequal game of reciprocities.'[8]

As for democratic equality, which, for different reasons, remains ever so misunderstood by both the Right and the Left, it must first be grasped as an intrinsically political notion. What democracy implies is the *political* equality of all citizens and not their 'natural' equality in any sort of way. As Carl Schmitt points out, 'the equality of everything "that bears a human face" is incapable of providing a foundation for a state, a state form or a form of government. No distinctive differentiations and delimitations may be derived from it; only the elimination of distinctions and boundaries may be. ... Nothing distinctive, either in religious or moral terms, or in political or economic ones, may be derived from the fact that all persons are human. ... The idea of human equality does not contain a juristic, a political, or an economic criterion. ... An equality with no other content than the equality that is alone common to all humans would be a non-political form of equality because it lacks the corresponding possibility of inequality. Any form of equality receives its significance and sense from the corresponding possibility of inequality. This equality becomes more intense as the inequality opposing it grows. A form of equality without the possibility of an inequality, an equality that one has exclusively and that cannot be at all lost, is without value and significance.'[9]

Just like any other political concept, democratic equality refers to the possibility of a distinction. It confirms a shared belonging to a specific political entity. The citizens of a democratic country enjoy equal political rights not because their skills are the same, but because they, too, are citizens of the country in question. Similarly, universal suffrage is not a confirmation of the intrinsic equality of voters (one man, one vote), nor is its purpose to render decisions on the truth. Instead,

8   Op. cit., page 186.

9   AN: Carl Schmitt, *Théorie de la constitution* (Constitutional Theory), PUF, Paris, 1993, pages 364–365.

it is a logical consequence of the fact that voters are also citizens, and its function is to express their preferences and make their agreement or disagreement known. Political equality, which acts as a prerequisite for all the other ones (indeed, in democracy, it is the people that embody the constituent power), is therefore in no way abstract: it is, instead, of the highest and most substantial importance. Even among the Greeks, *isonomia* has never implied that citizens are equal in nature or skill, nor even that everyone is equal before the law. What it alludes to instead is the fact that every citizen has the same capacity and right to participate in public life. Democratic equality therefore implies a common belonging, thereby contributing to the definition of a given identity. As for the term 'identity', it refers simultaneously to what distinguishes, i.e. to distinctiveness, and to what allows those who share this distinctiveness to identify each other. Carl Schmitt states:

> The word 'identity' signifies the existential quality of the political unity of the people, in contrast to any normative, schematic, or fictional types of equality.[10]

The first consequence that results from this is that 'the central concept of democracy is people and not humanity. If democracy is to be a political form at all, there is only a people's democracy and not that of humanity.'[11] The second consequence is that the corollary of the equality of citizens lies in their non-equality with those that are not citizens themselves. Schmitt writes once again:

> Political democracy, therefore, cannot rest on the inability to distinguish among persons, but rather only on the quality of belonging to a particular people. This quality of belonging to a people can be defined by very different elements (ideas of common race, belief, common destiny, and tradition). The equality that is part of the essence of democracy thus orients itself internally and not externally: within a democratic state system,

---

10   AN: Ibid., p. 372–373.
11   AN: Ibid., p. 371.

all members of the state are equal. The consequence for the political and public law perspective is that whoever is not a member of the state is not taken into account under this democratic equality.[12]

It is in this manner that 'such effects of democratic homogeneity demonstrate the opposition of democracy as a principle of political form to the liberal ideas of freedom and equality of the individual person with every other person. A democratic state would deprive itself of its substance through a logically consistent recognition of general human equality in the area of public life and of public law.'[13]

It would therefore be a grave mistake to contrast abstract equality with a simple notion of inequality. Indeed, inequality is not the opposite of equality, but its corollary: neither has any meaning in the absence of the other. The opposite of equality is actually incommensurability. Moreover, since one can only be equal or unequal as part of a given relation, there is no such thing as 'equal' or 'unequal' per se. A society where only inequality would reign is as unthinkable and inviable as one where only equality would prevail. For every society involves (and is bound to simultaneously involve) hierarchical relations and egalitarian ones, both of which are equally necessary to ensure its proper functioning. Julien Freund writes:

> Equality is one of the normal configurations of social relations, just like hierarchy itself. Egalitarianism, on the other hand, views all of these relations from the exclusive or predominant perspective of equality.[14]

To which he then adds:

> Egalitarianism is an ideological doctrine that would have us believe that there is a unique and universal relation capable of subsuming the various relations of equality that then engender a plurality of equalities ... A unique, exclusive and universal relationship would imply the existence

---

12   AN: Ibid., p. 365.

13   AN: Ibid., p. 371.

14   AN: Op. cit., p. 19.

of a point of view that would act as the reason behind all points of view. The very idea of a unique, exclusive and universal point of view, however, contradicts any notion of point of view.[15]

What is best about equality is actually known as 'reciprocity' and includes mutual assistance, specific solidarity, and a system of gifts and counter-gifts. One could say that, to some extent, equality and inequality melt into reciprocity.

The Ideology of Sameness

'I regard the history of the world, and that of societies, as being fully interpretable in accordance with two major principles: the principle of equalisation and that of differentiation (i.e. the propensity for similarity and the tendency to be different), which are always connected through constant relations of re-balancing, (genuine, fake, symbolic or real) compensation, or consolation', writes sociologist Paul Yonnet.[16]

I personally share this point of view, which is why I think that, lurking behind the egalitarian rhetoric, one must actually distinguish something else: a rising aspiration for homogeneity, for the resorption of all differences — the rise of what one could term the 'ideology of Sameness'.

The ideology of Sameness unfolds from what all men have in common. In fact, it unfurls by only taking into account their commonalities and interpreting them as being the Same. In the absence of a precise criterion allowing it to be assessed in a more specific manner, equality is but another way of referring to Sameness. The ideology of Sameness thus presents universal human equality as being equality per se, remaining disconnected from any concrete element that would actually make it possible to ascertain or invalidate such equality. To put things more simply, the ideology of Sameness surfaces as soon

15 AN: Ibid., p. 181–182

16 AN: Paul Yonnet, 'Diversité, différence' (Diversity and Difference), in *Une certaine idée* (A Certain Idea), 4th quarter 2000, page 94.

as equality is (wrongly) posited as a synonym for Sameness. It is an ideology that is allergic to anything that specifies, one which interprets any distinction as potentially devaluing and considers all differences to be incidental, transitory, inessential or secondary. Its driving force is the notion of the Unique, with the latter defined as anything that cannot bear otherness and that aims to reduce everything to a state of unity: one God, one civilisation, and one line of thought. Nowadays, the ideology of Sameness remains largely prevalent, acting simultaneously as the fundamental norm (in the Kelsenian sense of the *Grundnorm*[17]) — i.e. as one from which all the others stem — and the unique norm of a norm-less era refusing to experience any other norms.

This ideology is meant to be both descriptive and normative, since it presents the fundamental identity of all men as both an established fact and a desirable and achievable objective — without ever (or rarely) questioning the origin of the gap that separates the existing state of affairs from future reality. It thus seems to proceed from what actually is to what should be. In reality, however, it is on the basis of its own normativity, of its own conception of what should be, that it postulates an imaginary unitary being, a simple reflection of the mentality that inspires it.

Insofar as it emphasises the fundamental identity of individuals, of course, the ideology of Sameness comes up against everything that, in real life, actually sets them apart. It thus finds itself compelled to explain that these differences are but secondary and fundamentally insignificant specifications. Men may well differ in appearance, but are nonetheless essentially the same. Essence and existence are thus disconnected, as are the soul and the body, spirit and matter, and even rights and duties (the former stemming from the attributes of 'human

---

17   TN: The word *Grundnorm* is a German word translated as 'fundamental norm'. An Austrian jurist, legal philosopher and political philosopher, Hans Kelsen defined it as 'the postulated ultimate rule according to which the norms of this order are established and annulled, receiving or losing their validity'.

nature' and the latter only performed within a social relationship and in a specific context). Concrete existence is then nothing more than a deceptive embellishment, one that prevents you from perceiving the essential. It thus follows that the ideology of Sameness itself is not unitary in its postulate at all. Heir to both the Platonic myth of the cave and to the theological distinction between the created and the uncreated, it is dualistic in terms of structure and inspiration, in the sense that it can only convey the perspective of Sameness by relying on something that is foreign to diversity or that actually transcends it.

To eradicate diversity and guide humanity back to political and so-cial unity through its profane formulations, the ideology of Sameness usually resorts to theories that identify the social superstructure, the effects of domination, and the influence of upbringing or the environment as the very source of the distinctions that it regards as a transitory and temporary evil. (Note, in passing, that the theories in question identify the immediate causes of the state of affairs that they deplore, without ever wondering about the cause of these causes, that is to say, about their original source and the reasons why they never cease to re-emerge). Evil (*fons et origo malorum*[18]) is thus said to be external to man, as if the exterior were not, most and foremost, a product of the interior. By modifying the external causes, one could thus alter man's inner core, or even bring out his true 'nature'. In or-der to achieve this, one alternatively makes use of authoritarian and coercive methods, social conditioning or counter-conditioning, and 'dialogue' and 'appeals to reason', never achieving better results in one case than in the other and with failure always attributed not to errone-ous starting assumptions, but to the ever-insufficient character of the means employed. The underlying vision is that of a pacified or ideal society, or, at the very least, that of a society rendered 'just' as soon as one has removed the external contingencies that impede the advent of Sameness.

---

18   TN: The source and origin of our miseries.

The ideology of Sameness was initially formulated on a theological level, surfacing in the West through the Christian notion that all men, regardless of their personal characteristics and of the specific context of their actual existence, are endowed with a soul as part of an equal relationship with God. All men are thus, by their very nature, equal when it comes to the honour of having been created in the image of the one single God. And that is precisely why Christian society, no matter how diverse it may have managed to remain over the ages, revolves around a specific ideal, namely that of the Oneness of the collective body (and power). Hence this observation made by Hannah Arendt:[19]

> Such is the monotheistic representation of God — of God, in whose image man is supposed to have been created. Hence only *man* can exist, *men* only being, after all, a more or less successful repetition of the Same.[20]

The corollary, which was developed in great detail by Saint Augustine, is that of a humanity fundamentally defined as one single whole, all of whose elements are said to be destined to advance in the same direction by achieving an ever-increasing convergence. This is the Christian root of the notion of progress. When applied to our world on earth through the slow process of secularisation, this idea gives birth to that of a rationale that is common to all ('one complete whole in every one of us', Descartes would say), one that every man would partake in as a result of his very humanity. 'Thanks to this representation of a single world history', writes Hannah Arendt once again, 'the multiplicity of men is melted into *one single* human individual known as humanity.'[21]

---

19 TN: Regarded as one of the most influential political theorists of the 20th century, Hannah Arendt (14 October 1906–4 December 1975) was a political philosopher, author, and Holocaust survivor.

20 AN: Hannah Arendt, *Qu'est-ce que la politique?* (What Is Politics?), Seuil, Paris, 1995, p. 42.

21 AN: Ibid.

This here is, of course, not the right place for us to analyse the very manner in which the ideology of Sameness has given rise, within Western culture, to all those normative/repressive strategies described by Michel Foucault.[22] Let us simply bear in mind that over the course of its historical development, the nation-state has always been less concerned with integrating than with assimilating, that is to say, with the purpose of further reducing differences by standardising society as a whole. This process was taken further and accelerated by the French Revolution of 1789, a revolution which, ever faithful to geometrical logic, decreed the abolishment of all the intermediary bodies that the Old Regime had allowed to exist. Henceforth, one was merely willing to acknowledge the existence of humanity and, simultaneously, that of a citizenship whose very exercise is conceived of as one's participation in the universality of public affairs. Jews thus became 'citizens like any others' and women 'men like any others'. Whatever defined them specifically, be it their belonging to a given gender or to a given people, was deemed non-existent or required to be kept invisible by remaining confined to the private sphere. Marcel Gauchet[23] remarks:

> Spawned by the age of heteronomy, the configuration of Oneness would hence be destined to govern even the most extreme versions of autonomy. The preeminent commitment that the future will be imbued with is thus that of the restoration or establishment of collective unity … From this angle, the primary ideological concern can be summarised as follows: to find a way to generate the collective Oneness once produced by religion using non-religious means.[24]

The main modern ideologies would, in point of fact, alternatively fantasise about the unification of the world by means of the market,

---

22 TN: Paul-Michel Foucault (15 October 1926–25 June 1984) was a French philosopher, historian of ideas, author, political activist and literary critic.

23 TN: Born in 1946, Marcel Gauchet is a French historian, philosopher and sociologist.

24 AN: Marcel Gauchet, 'Croyances religieuses, croyances politiques' (Religious and Political Beliefs), in *Le Débat* (The Debate), May-August 2001, page 10.

about a 'homogeneous' society purged of all 'foreign' social negativity, and about a humanity that is at peace with itself, having at long last rediscovered all that defines its essence. The political ideal would thus be rooted in the gradual erasure of all those borders that arbitrarily separate men: we would thus call ourselves 'citizens of the world', as if the 'world' were (or could ever be) a political entity — which it is *not*.

The ideology of Sameness, however, did more than just lay the theoretical foundations of egalitarianism. Indeed, it also enabled the emergence of colonialism (in the name of the right of the most advanced ones on the road towards human convergence to bring about the 'progress' of those that were lagging behind on the path to progress), while simultaneously legitimising, within different states, the use of repression against all kinds of individuals that allegedly deviated from the 'general' standards. In the age of modernity, this tendency towards homogeneity was taken to the extreme in totalitarian societies by a central power asserting itself as the only possible source of legitimacy. And in Western post-modern societies, the same result has been achieved through the universalisation of the logic of profit and global commodification. It is a gentler yet more effective process: indeed, the degree of homogeneity characterising present-day Western societies greatly exceeds that of the totalitarian societies of the previous century.

The universalist ambition, which tends towards unity, always correlates with individualism, which, in turn, leads to separation and dissociation. The ideology that strives the most for the unification of the world is therefore also the very same one that triggers the greatest possible disunion. Such is the most flagrant contradiction engendered by the ideology of Sameness. The universalist aim is thus inevitably linked to individualism, as it can only present humanity as one fundamental whole by envisioning it as a composite of individual atoms, all of which are viewed as abstractly as possible, that is to say, completely out of context ('soil-less') and beyond all mediation, thus ultimately defined as both substitutable and interchangeable — which is why it aims to bring about the disappearance of all that separates the individual from humanity, namely popular cultures, intermediary bodies, and differentiated lifestyles. One thus readily understands the importance of not confusing the notion of difference with that of division. It is by eradicating differences and destroying the latter's very source, namely flexible structures (which also differ, and within which these differences fall), that the ideology of Sameness extends its hold. Targeting any differences organised in accordance with an organic principle, it simultaneously arouses fragmentation and division. In the absence of any integrative framework, the feverish excitement surrounding the ambition of Oneness leads to the dissolution of social cohesion.

It is thus perfectly logical that the rise of individualism, which liberals are ever so pleased with, has brought about the advent of the welfare state, whose emergence they now lament. The more community structures collapsed, the more the state had to take charge of people's protection. Conversely, the more it guaranteed their protection, the more it exempted them from 'maintaining family-related or community-related ties that had previously been the source of indispensable protections',[25] thus fostering assistantship and irresponsibility. A dialectical movement and vicious circle thus ensue: on the one hand, our differentiated society is now unravelling, and on the other, the homogenising state is advancing at the same pace as individualism itself. The greater the number of isolated individuals, the more uniformly they are treated by the state.

In constant competition and opposition with each other, the great modern ideologies have, as a result of their clashes, further aggravated the divisions and dissociations triggered by the spread of individualism. This paradoxical result has, however, only served to stimulate them in their ambition: faced with the spectre of 'anarchy' and 'social

---

25   AN: Marcel Gauchet, *La religion dans la démocratie. Parcours de la laïcité* (Religion in Democracy — The Journey of Secularism), Gallimard, Paris, 1998, pages 68–69.

dissolution', with class struggle, civil war and social anomie, they argued with even greater ardour in favour of present alignment and future levelling. Once again, Marcel Gauchet remarks:

> Even those who strive to highlight the very scope and inexpiable character of the antagonisms plaguing their contemporary societies do so in order to emphasise, by means of contrast, the promise to resolve the contradictions held by the future. This is typical of Marx. Bearing witness to the convulsions and heartbreaks of the present thus only strengthens one's faith in, and hope for, the coming unity.[26]

The problem is that the ideology of Sameness is bound to demand the radical exclusion of all that cannot be reduced to such Sameness. Irreconcilable otherness thus becomes the primary enemy, one that must be eradicated once and for all. Such is the motivation of all totalitarian ideologies — the elimination of all those 'redundant men' who, owing to their very existence, impede the advent of a homogeneous society or unified world. Whosoever speaks in the name of 'humanity' inevitably excludes his adversaries from it.

The contradictory logic espoused by both universalism and individualism is not the only contradiction that shapes the ideology of Sameness. In its argumentations, for instance, the latter either proceeds from the idea of 'human nature' (one that has been reconstructed in accordance with its own postulates, of course) or from the assertion that all natural characteristics are secondary and that man could never embrace his own humanity more faithfully than by freeing himself from these incidental characteristics. Not only do these two statements contradict each other, but the second is also at odds with scientistic ideology, according to which man can be entirely regarded as any other natural object, so much so that 'there is nothing about him which natural sciences could, one day, fail to unveil'.[27]

---

26 AN: As stated in the above-mentioned article.

27 AN: Alain Supiot, 'La fonction anthropologique du droit' (The Anthropological Function of Rights), in *Esprit*, February 2001, page 153.

The corollary of abstract equality is the principle of non-difference. The logical consequence is that if all men are equal, all their opinions are equally valid — hence contemporary relativism and the liberal theory of the necessary neutrality of the state with regard to all that pertains to values and purposes (the 'good life' defined by Aristotle). This neutrality can only be apparent, however, because the mere fact of choosing to be neutral is, in itself, not neutral at all. In addition to this, it is obvious that liberals do not recognise antiliberal theories as having the same value as liberal ones. And obviously enough, the opinion according to which all opinions are equal does not prevent anyone from rallying against certain opinions, beginning with the one according to which not all opinions are equal.[28]

There is, of course, a contradiction between planetary homogenisation and the fact of championing the cause of all peoples, which implies the recognition and preservation of their plurality. We cannot, therefore, defend both the ideal of a unified world and the right of all peoples to shape their own destiny, as there is nothing to guarantee that they will shape it in accordance with this very ideal. Similarly, one cannot advocate pluralism — defined as the legitimisation and recognition of all differences — while arguing in favour of equal conditions, which would result in the reduction of these differences. Last but not least, if the earth is indeed only populated by people who are 'equal to each other', what is the use of asserting the inalienable rights of each and every individual? How can one praise both what makes us unique and irreplaceable and what is said to make us virtually interchangeable? One could, admittedly, evade the issue through various slogans involving mental pirouettes, as in 'equality in difference'. Such an expression, however, makes no sense at all, for it only refers to non-differentiating 'difference'. One cannot support people's right to be different while simultaneously believing that that which unites men in Sameness is fundamentally more defining with regard to their

---

28 AN: See the book written by Philippe Béneton on the topic, entitled *Les fers de l'opinion* (The Shackles of Opinion) and published by PUF, Paris, in 2000.

social identity than what distinguishes them from one another. Pietro Barcellona[29] was thus absolutely right when using the expression 'the tragedy of equality' to describe the paradox according to which one can, by resorting to the notion of equality, simultaneously invalidate all forms of hierarchy and guarantee 'diversity or what makes individuals unique'.

Ethnocentrism or the Principle of Diversity

Just as it would be pointless to contrast abstract equality with an equally abstract notion of inequality, it would, in my opinion, be wrong to attempt to do so when it comes to nationalism/ethnocentrism and the ideology of Sameness — for what the former have historically achieved on a small scale, the ideology of Sameness has accomplished on a larger one. And both remain, above all else, confined to what Heidegger rightly termed 'the metaphysics of subjectivity', which he defines as the most essential trait of modernity.

Nationalism and ethnocentrism regard peoples and nations in the same way liberalism perceives individuals: as essentially 'free' beings, deriving their rights and numerous attributes from their unlimited 'freedom' and only compelled to abide by their own will, within the framework of selfish acts and the fulfilment of their best interest. Envisioned as absolute freedom of action and as a situation in which one would depend on nothing else, the independence to which they both aspire is itself modelled on the liberal ideal of individual autonomy, thus allowing for prompt decisions in accordance with one's will. Viewed from this perspective, the universal struggle of peoples and nations is only a projection of inter-individual competition on a vaster scale, one where the tribunal of history plays the role of the market. The dogma of state sovereignty is also linked to the metaphysics of subjectivity, displaying, in the final analysis, a tendency towards solipsism, which places the individual and the self at the centre of the

---

29 TN: Pietro Barcellona (1936–2013) was an Italian teacher, politician and philosopher.

world and defines the latter as merely the object of the 'I's' will and self-representation. The only difference here is that the 'I' is replaced by a 'we' — for every ethnocentric people is only interested in itself.

Ethnocentric peoples only assess events and situations in accordance with the positive or negative developments they can expect from them. These words obviously only make sense in the context of the denial of all justice and truth — which also goes against the notion of organicism, because the very principle of organicism is one of democratic solidarity and social reciprocity, as opposed to the principle of association on the sole basis of common interests. Just as universalism is never anything but an inflated sort of ethnocentrism reaching for the very borders of the universe, nationalism is nothing more than collective individualism. What is disregarded in both cases is the very meaning of specific particularity and universality.

Ethnocentrism is, furthermore, rooted in a flawed conception of the notion of identity. Indeed, an identity is not an essence, but a substance that is to be 'constructed' on a daily basis. It is thus not to be defined as something that never changes, but rather as something that must be kept ever-present through change. Last but not least, it is always 'reflexive', meaning that the very formation of one's self is always channelled through exchanges with others. And that is why any defence of identities can, in truth, only be conducted on the basis of one's understanding of otherness.

Just like universalism, ethnocentrism is allergic to Others and is always prone to regard them as being 'redundant'. The only difference is that ethnocentrism is more brutal by comparison. Universalism tends to deny otherness by reducing Others to a state of Sameness, while ethnocentrism tends to curtail diversity by eliminating otherness or keeping it uncompromisingly away. As part of both attitudes, otherness is considered devoid of interest and diversity worthless. Conversely, a positive conception of otherness consists in acknowledging differences without using them as an argument to demand that some people relinquish their existence and submit to the desires, interests or motivations of others. Not only does oppression deny the freedom of the oppressed, but also that of the oppressors themselves. That is precisely what Marx meant when he wrote that 'a people which oppresses another cannot emancipate itself'. We are all familiar with the dialectic of the master and the slave: the two roles are inevitably reversed at some point. Indeed, those that have colonised others should not be surprised when they, too, are eventually colonised. He who destroys the identity of others does not strengthen his, but makes it more vulnerable, endangering it further in a world that has, yet again, lost some of its diversity.

It is, in fact, the principle of diversity that one should contrast with the ideology of Sameness. Indeed, every principle draws its strength from its general character. The diversity of the world is its only true wealth, for it acts as the foundation of the most precious of assets: identity. And neither peoples nor people are actually interchangeable. To say that none bear within themselves any more or any less value than others is not tantamount to saying that they are the same (considering Sameness in its various forms), but that they are, in fact, all different. Tolerance does not consist in looking at Others so as to perceive this Sameness in them, but in doing so in order to understand what they are comprised of in terms of otherness, i.e. to grasp what otherness really is, namely a reality that cannot be reduced to any sort of 'understanding' through mere self-projection. Differentialism does not prohibit you from making value judgements, nor does it condemn anyone to truth-ignorant relativism. What it does, however, is ban one from languishing mentally in an abstract overhanging position and from portraying oneself as a dominant authority (due to the latter's alleged 'universality' or 'superiority'), by virtue of which it becomes possible, even necessary, to impose upon other peoples a way of life that is not theirs. When Plato states that the best form of government is one in which all citizens participate in both enforced and endured domination,[30] he certainly sets out a general principle that reaches well beyond the borders of the Greek city-state, yet he does not exclude the possibility of different peoples adopting different laws.

It is not a question of falling into naïve idealism, as identities can still clash with one another, and differences assert themselves at the expense of others. Under such circumstances, it is perfectly normal to defend one's own (ethnic) belonging above all else. Defending one's identity against the abusive self-affirmation of others (through colonisation, mass immigration, etc.) and considering it to be the only worthwhile one are, however, two very different matters. Although the principle of diversity is not undermined by the first attitude, the same cannot be said of the second.

Likewise, it is not a question of moving from one excess to another by prioritising differences so much that one becomes oblivious to common aspects. It is just that differences are more important — firstly, because they are the ones that specify, define an identity, and make each person or people irreplaceable, and secondly, because a person's belonging to humanity is never immediate, but on the contrary, always mediate: one is only human to the extent that one belongs to one of humanity's constituent cultures or communities. (It was Joseph de Maistre[31] who once said: 'I have seen men of all kinds, but never in my life have I encountered man himself'). Last but not least, differences are more significant because it is by means of particularness that one can access the universal, and not the other way around, as the latter process could only consist in deducing an abstract notion of singularity from a concept of the universal that one has formulated in advance. All concrete existence thus proves to be inseparable from a particular context, from one or more specific affiliations. All belonging is most certainly a limitation, but a limitation that delivers us from others. Dreaming of the unconditional is, after all, still dreaming.

---

30 AN: Republic VIII, 11, 557c.

31 TN: Joseph de Maistre was a Savoyard philosopher, who was also active as an author, solicitor and diplomat.

'Men are afraid of Sameness, and therein lies the source of racism', remarked Jean-Pierre Dupuy.[32] To which he then added: 'What men are afraid of is undifferentiation, for the latter is always a sign and product of social disintegration ... Equality, whose very principle is to negate differences, gives rise to mutual dread.'[33] Men are indeed afraid of Sameness, at least as much, if not more, than of Otherness.

In a display of irenic naiveté, dominant ideologies believe that the homogenisation of the world could only have a pacifying effect, because it allegedly enables better 'understanding'. On the contrary, however, we can all see how it arouses identitarian tensions, awakens secular irredentism, and engenders nationalistic upheavals. At the very core of societies, furthermore, the ideology of Sameness has given birth to widespread emulative rivalry, a rivalry which René Girard[34] described so very accurately and that exacerbates the desire to distinguish oneself from others with all the more fervour, since it actually prohibits distinctions. Sameness thus turns out to be a source of profound conflict. At its best, it results in widespread indifference and boredom; at its worst, it leads to violent reactions and inflames people's emotions.

The incommensurability of people and cultures is, however, not synonymous with incommunicability. Indeed, it only implies the recognition of what irreducibly distinguishes them from one another. As for the ideology of Sameness, it aspires to complete transparency, despite the fact that the social always implies an opaque aspect, with opacity itself rooted in the incommensurable. There are some — mostly those who automatically interpret identity as confinement — who believe that asserting differences can only make men increasingly foreign to one another, but it is the opposite that is actually true, for every exchange presupposes otherness. An exchange only makes

32   TN: Now 81 years old, Jean-Pierre Dupuy is a French philosopher and engineer.

33   AN: 'Différences et inégalités' (Differences and Inequalities), in *Découverte* (Discovery), Paris, 1984.

34   TN: René Noël Théophile Girard (25 December 1923–4 November 2015) was a French polymath, historian, literary critic and philosopher of social science.

sense to the extent that it contributes to something in the presence of another. Exchanging the Same for the Same can only occur in monologues. Dialogue and 'dialogism' (a term proposed by Martin Buber[35]) both imply otherness — otherwise, any dialogue is reduced to a monologue. Not only does the preservation of differences not prevent dialogue and exchange, but it is, in fact, their primary condition. In this respect, it would be a mistake to contrast difference, purported to be aggressive and elitist, with diversity, for diversity is nothing but an arrangement of harmonised differences. A society only comprised of men 'like any others' would inevitably be one where individuals have become interchangeable to such a point that the disappearance or elimination of any one of them would, from a broad societal perspective, only take on a relative sort of importance. The situation is, by contrast, quite the opposite in a differentiated society. Difference is, furthermore, a resistance factor, and therefore one of freedom. If individuals and peoples were basically the same, or were completely mouldable, it would increase their vulnerability to the threat of propaganda and conditioning. However, the very fact that their diversity resurfaces on a regular basis and that mankind is highly polymorphic proves that they are anthropologically resistant to homogenising models. Last but not least, difference is an element of integration and harmony. Societies that acknowledge the existence and importance of differences are also the ones most capable of integrating those characterised by such differences (in the past, even the village idiot had his place in the village). Societies that fail to recognise differences or that regard them as insignificant are, on the other hand, doomed either to exclude those who do not fit into the unique pattern that one seeks to impose or to bring about the disintegration of social cohesion by draining it of its organic, composite and differentiated character.

---

35 TN: Martin Buber (8 February 1878–13 June 1965) was an Austrian Jewish and Israeli philosopher famous for his philosophy of dialogue.

The Rebirth of Identities

The history of modernity can be conceived of, at least in part, as a colossal process of standardisation. Triggered by philosophical-moral and/or political universalism, as well as by the spread of techniques whose very effectiveness in terms of shaping behaviours is greater than that of the most centralised kind of dictatorship, it resulted in the gradual eradication of differentiated lifestyles in the West, and in the Third World in acculturation and the imposition of the Western myth of 'development'. This process seems to have reached its peak with the rise of globalisation. The ideology of Sameness is now 'all-encompassing' (to use the term proposed by Paul Virilio[36]), insofar as it tends to give birth to a world *that lacks any sort of exterior* and in which flows travel in all directions in 'zero time'. Both 'pluralism' and even the 'multiculturalism' to which people attach such great importance today are no more than the shadow and caricature of the particularisms of old, particularisms that are now disappearing beneath a veneer of increasingly homogeneous tendencies and behaviours. In Western countries, people already dress, eat, talk, take up residence, entertain themselves, live and even think in an increasingly similar way. They consume the same products, watch the same performances and listen to the same music. Specific cultures linked to a particular professional, political or religious affiliation have all but disappeared. Regional cultures and languages are also endangered. The lifestyles we have inherited from the past are only preserved for the purpose of tourist entertainment and intended to generate added value. They are all but frozen memories, traditions that are maintained artificially, and recollections that relate to folklore or museography. The only remaining differences have to do with one's level of income: although they impact quantity, they change little in terms of the very nature of people's choices and aspirations (regardless of the social class people

---

36 TN: Paul Virilio (4 January 1932–10 September 2018) was a French cultural theorist, aesthetic philosopher and urbanist.

belong to, they all want the same thing). At the same time, any project that deviates from the dominant norm is rejected as a dangerous utopia or harmful thought in the name of one-track thinking. As for our entire media system, it is set to praise the current state of affairs, implicitly presented as being the best (or the least harmful) of all possible worlds, perhaps even as the only possible world. Since its primary function is to justify people's adaptation to the standards of unlimited consumption, it strives to 'homogenise needs, demands, expectations and desires'.[37] Despite the ever-growing economic and social disparities, the planet is unified within a single economic and moral framework: on the one hand, the ideology of 'human rights', and on the other, the monotheistic adulation of the market.

In a world characterised by a widespread crisis afflicting our institutions and major systems of social integration, by the collapse of the nation-state model and the growing insignificance of territorial borders, what we are simultaneously witnessing is the re-emergence of a tremendous thirst for re-rooting, a thirst that is channelled through the shaping of communities and networks. Spontaneously, civil society is restructuring itself and re-establishing groups and 'tribes' that seek to remedy the growing lack of role differentiation, the widespread circulation of countless goods and the systematic disappearance of basic social skills by reintroducing otherness into people's daily and local lives and resorting to direct democracy and the principle of subsidiarity. Thanks to its rapid and almost 'viral' spread, this phenomenon has proven single-handedly that we have already exited modernity. The successor of people's desire for freedom, the desire for equality was the greatest passion of the modern age. As for the greatest passion of our post-modern era, it shall be none other than the desire for identity.

This post-modern preoccupation often takes on the shape of a desire to have one or several aspects of collective belonging (all of which are regarded as constitutive of identity) recognised in the public

---

37 AN: Pierre-André Taguieff, *Marianne*, 21 May 2001, page 68.

sphere, and no longer only in the private one, to which modernity had confined them in the name of republican universalism, of a demand for 'assimilation' or an ideal of axiological 'neutrality'. Regardless of the types of belonging that this claim relates to (cultural, ethnic, linguistic, regional, religious, sexual, etc.; inherited or chosen; lasting or transitory), the fact remains that it is no longer primarily tolerance that is sought, but recognition and respect. Whereas the purpose of the nation-state was the tendential abolishment of all distinctions and intermediary bodies that prevented it from being the sole incarnation of the social whole and the guarantor of the latter's unity, it is now a matter of recognising associations and communities insofar as they abide by common law (which is obviously not the case with the various kinds of so-called 'communitarianism' that stem from immigration and which, having established themselves in the shape of counter-societies, thus constitute yet another form of social pathology) and of allowing them to continually develop in a self-sustainable manner, either because they are, by their very nature, impossible to influence through political management or because their main purpose is to exist as they are. Far from necessarily striving to espouse an inward-looking attitude, good communities long to become full members of society by and large. This simultaneously contradicts any political model that can only envision a social contract concluded among individuals that have nothing in common in the first place. The growing significance of the issue of identity in post-modern democracies thus encourages us to open up the sphere of political democracy to collective identities as such. As a result of this, identity is becoming, once again, one of the primary conditions for the practical exercise of citizenship.

The modern age was an era marked by a total mobilisation of the masses, with the latter having replaced the evangelisation of peoples. As for the post-modern era, it encourages the assertiveness of dispersed identities, both on the individual level and that of communities themselves. This trend is not, however, devoid of ambiguity.

Regardless of the fact that it takes place against a backdrop of unprecedented social homogenisation (involving the end of the peasantry, the disappearance of household servants, the vanishing of working-class conditions, the ever-increasing alignment of masculine-feminine social roles, etc.), it sometimes encompasses a certain 'pluralism' that bears hardly any relation to genuine diversity. A typical example of such false pluralism is the increase in the number of different brands to market the same product. More generally, false pluralism is the kind that reduces the democratic game to the competitive action of established pressure groups. The rise in the number of micro-differences, of factitious or superficial ones, can create an illusion of pluralism while simultaneously causing us to lose sight of the deep meaning of the notion of difference. The very idea that one people or another can espouse a worldview, a way of experiencing its presence in the world in a radically different way from ours, thus gradually becomes incomprehensible.

Post-modern identities, on the other hand, differ quite markedly from traditional ones. They have lost some of their 'naturalness' or 'objectivity'. Marcel Gaucher remarks:

> Any order genuinely rooted in customs, one that is experienced as having been passed down in its entirety, is an a-subjective order in relation to the identity of those that are part of it and implement it. [Nowadays, however,] the very opposite occurs: the adoption of collective characteristics acts as the vector of personal singularity. Your belonging is subjectivising because it is asserted and cultivated for the very subjectification it produces.[38]

In other words, identities are henceforth less perceived as objective data than they are considered to be the result of one's subjective decision. Owing to their anteriority/authority, past affiliations were adopted in the absence of genuine choice. Today, however, even inherited affiliations are also chosen ones, insofar as they only take effect when

---

38   AN: *La religion dans la démocratie*, op. cit., page 92.

we decide to identify with them. They thus have no power except for the one that we consent to grant them.

The primary issue, in fact, has not changed at all: it is still a matter of finding out whether the ideology of Sameness will ultimately prevail. And this is precisely where I agree with what I myself wrote back in 1977, in my introduction to *View from the Right*:

> What is the principal menace today? It is the progressive demise of the world's diversity.

Nowadays, one rightly stresses the importance of biodiversity. The latter, however, must encompass more than just animal and plant species — indeed, it goes without saying that it must also apply to both cultures and peoples.

IRREPLACEABLE COMMUNITIES

WHETHER ANCIENT OR RECENT, of an ethno-cultural, linguistic, religious, sexual or any other kind, communities are a natural aspect of one's belonging. No individual can exist without affiliations, even when distancing himself from them. The 'I' is always situated somewhere, that is to say, incorporated into a story — a story that can never be reduced to a status quo, much less to some kind of past. A community is a social form that precedes society, just as it precedes man (when viewed separately, as a single individual). It is present before the birth of the state, before the emergence of any institution, bringing together those closest, the similar ones, as part of families organised in tribes, prior to their gathering in cities. Even language itself is a factual aspect of community — which implies the presence of a community of speakers capable of understanding each other. Likewise, any 'we' — or 'we-ness' — precedes every 'I'. A community, by definition, stems from sharing and common experience. Francis Cousin[1] writes:

> Man is a community being not as a result of external and subsequent contingencies, but because of a dialectic of intimate and prerequisite historical necessity. The human dimension represents, genetically speaking, the very being of my conscious community. In other words, as soon as man

---

1   TN: Francis Cousin is a French author.

emerges, the 'community of the we' and the 'reality of the I' appear indis-
solubly unified within one single synthetic whole.[2]

The notion of community is as old as political philosophy, since it
goes back to at least Aristotle. Traditionally, the opponents of liberal individualism have always adhered to a conception of the social
phenomenon that leans towards community rather than society.
The dichotomy between community and society has been studied
by many authors, beginning with Ferdinand Tönnies, who, in his
famous work published in 1887, presented community and society as
'two fundamental categories of pure sociology', interpreting human
history as that of the gradual replacement of the community model
by a societal one.[3] A precursor to Louis Dumont's work on holism
and individualism, Tönnies demonstrated that the individual is not
an immediate datum that one would encounter in any social organ-
isation, but a notion linked to a particular social form, namely that
of the *Gesellschaft* (society), which contrasts point by point with the
Gemeinschaft (community).

A community results in a form of organic sociality, and society
in a 'mechanical' type of relationship founded on the prevalence of
the individual. A *Gemeinschaft* constitutes a whole whose scope
exceeds that of its parts: in it, solidarity and mutual aid sprout from
the notion of the common good, and not common goods that are
distributed equally among all. It is a common good whose enjoyment
predates sharing from the very outset. By contrast, in the model of the
Gesellschaft (a conception of which is already present, albeit in em-
bryonic form, in the theory of the social contract), men live together

---

2   AN: Francis Cousin, *L'être contre l'avoir* (Being versus Having), Le Retour aux
     Sources, 2012, page 82. On the topic of the 'community of habitus' or people's
     dispositions, see also Olivier Ducharme's *Michel Henry et le problème de la
     communauté* (Michel Henry and the Issue of Community), L'Harmattan, Paris,
     2013.

3   AN: Ferdinand Tönnies, *Communauté et société* (Community and Society),
     PUF, Paris, 2010.

without genuine solidarity or unity. A society is thus defined as no more than a gathering of individuals. It was, in fact, in favour of the previous conception that Abbé Sieyès[4] declared himself to be when making the following statement at the time of the Revolution:

> We will never understand this social mechanism if we do not undertake to analyse society as if it were an ordinary machine, examining each of its parts separately before mentally re-connecting them all, one by one, in order to grasp its tuning principles and hear the general harmony that inevitably results from this.[5]

Instead of resulting from the consensual effect of an 'organic will' (*Wesenwille*), the social cohesion of the modern era stems from 'rational will' (*Kürwille*): the members of a society thus decide to live together not because they share the same values, but because of a common interest in this regard. More specifically, 'social' relations are simply reduced to legal agreements or commercial exchange. Here is what Tönnies wrote in reference to society:

> On the contrary, everyone is out for himself alone and living in a state of tension against everyone else. The various spheres of power and activity are sharply demarcated, so that everyone resists contact with others and excludes them from his own spheres, regarding any such overtures as hostile. Such a *negative* attitude is the normal and basic way in which these power-conscious people relate to one another, and it is characteristic of a *Gesellschaft* at any given moment in time. Nobody wants to do anything for anyone else; nobody wants to yield or give anything unless he gets something in return that he regards as at least an *equal* trade-off. ... Only the prospect of a profit would lead one to give up a property that he possesses ... While in a *Gemeinschaft* they remain linked in spite of distinctions, here they remain distinct despite all the links.

---

4   TN: Abbé Sieyès was a Roman Catholic clergyman and political author.

5   AN: Siéyès, *Qu'est-ce que le Tiers État?* (What Is the Third Estate?), Société de l'histoire de la Révolution française, Paris, 1888, page 65.

To which he then adds that 'the big city, and society in general, represents the corruption and death of the people'.

Although Tönnies has sometimes been accused of espousing 'romanticism' in his theories, it is necessary to understand that the notions he contests in a term-to-term fashion are 'ideal types' (as defined by Max Weber[6]) — for there is no such thing as a community or society 'in the absolute sense of the term'. Indeed, every human network possesses, albeit in varying proportions, both community traits and 'societal' ones. What one must actually bear in mind regarding the notion of community is the latter's exceedingly organic character compared to that of a society. This organicism is not, of course, to be taken in a strictly biological sense, but in a metaphorical one: inside a body, organs are not identical, but, instead, simultaneously different and complementary.[7]

As an organic phenomenon, a community entails, on all levels, the implementation of a principle of finality (the common good, which cannot be reduced to efficient causality) and of the principle of subsidiarity as defined by Johannes Althusius[8] in the 16th century. In contrast with the state sovereignty established by Jean Bodin,[9] who

---

6   TN: Considered one of the most important theoreticians of the development of modern Western society, Maximilian Karl Emil Weber (21 April 1864–14 June 1920) was a German sociologist, historian, jurist, and political economist.

7   AN: 'The organic has a *unifying* dimension, insofar as it rests on a structuring vision of the social body. As such, it characterises a society whose members are connected to each other in a life-sustaining manner (just like the organs of the human body) with a view to cooperating for the common good, for the good of the entire body', writes Marie-Pauline Deswarte in one of her books, whose sole flaw is that of excessively idealising the Old Regime (*La République organique en France. Un patrimoine constitutionnel à restaurer,* V [The Organic Republic in France. Restoring a Constitutional Heritage, V]). See also 'Retrouver la dynamique organique de la France' (Rediscovering the Organic Dynamics of France) by the same author, in *Valeurs actuelles,* 8 January 2015, page 79.

8   TN: Johannes Althusius (1563–12 August 1638) was a German jurist and political philosopher.

9   AN: In *The Republic,* 1576.

called for a separation between political and civil society, as well as for the elimination of intermediary bodies, Althusius defines the *res publica* as a layering of both 'simple and private communities' (families, schools and corporations) and 'mixed and public communities' (cities and provinces) that are crowned by a 'higher political community', with each level granted as much freedom as possible to make its own decisions in all matters that concern it. Characterised as 'symbiotic', politics is thus the art of enabling people to live in a community, with sovereignty (*majestas*) divided among all the levels of the social body.[10]

And that is precisely why the community model goes so well with integral federalism, which grants intermediary bodies and the principle of subsidiarity a major role. The notion of 'intermediary bodies' does not, of course, refer solely to the corporations of the Old Regime, the abolition of which (as a result of the Revolution) left individuals isolated in the face of the state, while, at the same time, justifying the prohibition of labour coalitions and trade unions. Pierre Dardot[11] and Christian Laval[12] write:

> Only on the basis of cooperation could one ever create a federation involving different municipalities, peoples or production activities. In other words, when properly understood, the federative principle implies a denial of the very foundations of capitalism.[13]

---

10 AN: See Alain de Benoist's 'Johannes Althusius, 1557–1638', in *Krisis*, Paris, 22 March 1999, pages 2–34, and Jean-Sylvestre Mongrenier's 'Johannes Althusius et l'Europe subsidiaire' (Johannes Althusius and Subsidiary Europe), online text, 25 June 2009.

11 TN: Pierre Dardot is a philosopher who focuses particularly on Hegel and Marx.

12 TN: Christian Laval is an author and a professor of sociology at the Université de Paris Ouest Nanterre La Défense.

13 AN: Pierre Dardot and Christian Laval, *Commun. Essai sur la révolution du XXIe siècle* (Common — An Essay on the Revolution of the 21st Century), La Découverte, Paris, 2014, page 461.

As for federalism itself, it stems from the model of the empire, which, throughout history, represented the main political form rivalling that of the nation-state. The primary characteristic of the notion of empire, whose oldest theoreticians were Marsilius of Padua, Dante and Nicholas of Cusa, lies, above all, in its aim — that of highlighting differences. In an empire, sovereignty is divided and shared; ethnic, cultural, religious and traditional particularities legally recognised (provided that they do not violate common law); and the principle of subsidiarity implemented as the supreme rule. Indeed, since nationality is not synonymous with citizenship, the political people (*demos*) is not to be confused with the ethnic one (*ethnos*), though one does not preclude the other. Today, one will readily notice how 'republicans' reduce nationality to citizenship, with the proponents of an ethnic conception of the nation adopting the opposite approach, as both groups remain trapped in the same inability to distinguish the two concepts. Historically, the philosophy of the Enlightenment began by targeting organic communities, whose way of life it denounced as being imbued with irrational 'superstitions' and 'prejudices', all in a desire to replace them with a society of individuals. The central idea was that individuals exist not on the basis of their affiliations, but independently of them, as part of an abstract notion involving a 'disengaged' subject (or 'unencumbered self') that predates its own ends, serving as a basis for the ideology of human rights. Carried forth by a lay version of the ideology of Sameness, the modern theory that defines mankind as uprooted or severed from all tradition thus saw the light of day.

Liberalism regards men as being interchangeable because it only perceives them in an abstractly generic way, as soilless beings disconnected from any sort of community and devoid of any belonging, with such severance viewed as the primary condition for their 'emancipation'. Likewise, liberalism only concerns itself with 'freedom of choice', and not with the empirical consequences of such choices (indeed, even wrong choices are always justified, provided that they were made freely). In the eyes of liberals, the notion of the common good is meaningless, because there is no specific entity with the potential to benefit from it: since every society only consists of individuals, there is no 'good' that could ever be common to its members. 'Social good' can, in other words, only be understood as a simple aggregate of individual good, resulting from the choices made by individuals.[14] It was in this respect that Margaret Thatcher stated that 'there is no such thing as society'.[15]

In a more general sense, it is all of modernity that has been constructed in harmony with a theory based on the existence of individuals that could only be said to be 'free and equal in terms of rights' because they were considered free or severed from any and all community affiliations. This position is constantly reiterated by the philosophy of the Enlightenment whenever the latter contrasts reason with tradition, civilisation with nature, and universalism with specific cultures, assuring us that the freedom and aptitude of individuals depend on them being torn away from all familial, cultural or religious roots. Such was the very programme espoused in recent times by Vincent Peillon, the French Minister of National Education, when he declared that the role of schools was to 'snatch students away from all forms of familial, ethnic, social, and intellectual determinism'.

As for Marx, according to whom man is defined as the sum of all of his social relations, he agrees with Aristotle when characterising man as a political, social and community-based animal (*zoón politikon*).

14 AN: The highly libertarian Ayn Rand thus writes: 'The tribe (or the public or society) is only a number of individual men. Nothing can be good for the tribe as such.' (*Capitalism. The Unknown Ideal*, Penguin, New York, 1986, p. 20).

15 AN: At the time of the Scottish independence referendum (September 2014), Geraldine Vaughan, a lecturer in British history and civilisation at the University of Rouen, explained that those who were in favour of independence demanded it because of their hostility to liberal individualism: 'The Thatcherite ideology has clashed with Scottish values deeply rooted in the notion of community. The praise of individualism has neither been understood nor accepted. Thatcher's neo-liberal policies have all but destroyed the welfare state — which has been perceived as an attack against the communitarian idea. The ideological and moral gap separating her from the Scots has thus widened.'

His opinion is thus in line with that of all those who have, throughout the history of human thought, challenged the liberal conception according to which man is but an isolated atom solely connected to others through the interplay of individual interests. As written by François Flahault,[16] 'the social interdependence of individuals is not utilitarian, but ontological'.[17] Indeed, legal and mercantile relations are not enough to establish a good society.

It is within this roughly outlined context that one must situate the appearance and development of the communitarian current in Anglo-Saxon countries, starting in the early 1980s with prominent representatives such as Alasdair MacIntyre, Charles Taylor and Michael Sandel. The aim of this school of thought was to formulate a new theory that closely combines moral philosophy with political philosophy, a theory which was, at the very beginning, developed, on the one hand, on the basis of the specific situation experienced by the United States, where one witnessed a real rise in the 'policies of (human) rights', and, on the other, in response to the liberal political theories that had been reformulated by authors such as Ronald Dworkin, Bruce Ackerman and especially John Rawls during the previous decade.[18]

---

16   TN: In addition to being a writer, François Flahault is a senior researcher and a member of the Centre de Recherches sur les Arts et le Langage (Art and Language Research Centre).

17   AN: François Flahault, *Pourquoi limiter l'expansion du capitalisme?* (Why Limit the Expansion of Capitalism?), Descartes & Cie, Paris, 2003, page 92.

18   AN: The English word 'communitarianism' was first used in 1841 by John Goodwyn Barmby, the founder of the Universal Communitarian Association. It should be noted that the communitarian movement has greatly evolved since its beginnings, with some of its representatives, including Michael Sandel, having since relinquished such a label, and others having partially adopted new positions under the impact of liberal criticism. For a recent update, see Amitai Etzioni's 'Communitarianism Revisited', published in the *Journal of Political Ideologies*, October 2014, pages 241–260. As for earlier publications on the topic, they include Shlomo Avineri and Avner de-Shalit's (ed.) *Communitarianism and Individualism*, Oxford University Press, Oxford, 1992; Elizabeth Frazer's *The Problem of Communitarian Politics*, Oxford University Press, Oxford,

It was, first and foremost, by drawing on Tönnies' work, while also embracing a salutary return to the ideas of Aristotle, that the communitarian school endeavoured to demonstrate the fictional character of liberal anthropology, which is rooted in a theory of subjective rights ('human rights') and the notion of an individual that precedes his own ends, i.e. one that exercises choice in a rational manner and out of any socio-historical context, thus defining himself as a utility-driven consumer displaying unlimited needs.

The main reproach that communitarians target liberal individualism with is specifically that it results in the disappearance of communities, which are a fundamental and irreplaceable element of human existence. Liberalism devalues political life by considering political association to be a mere instrumental good, lacking the ability to see that the involvement of citizens in the political community is an intrinsic good that acts as an essential feature of a good life. It is therefore unable to satisfactorily analyse and explain a certain number of obligations and commitments, including those that do not result from voluntary choice or contractual commitment such as family obligations and the need to serve one's country or give general interest priority over personal gain. It propagates an erroneous conception of the 'I' by refusing to acknowledge the fact that the latter is always 'embedded' in a given socio-historical context and, at least in part, comprised of values and commitments that are neither subject to individual choice nor revocable at will. Furthermore, it leads to an exaggerated version of the policy of (human) rights, a policy that has henceforth little to do with legality itself, as well as to a new type of institutional system, namely the 'procedural republic'. Last but not least, it disregards, as a result of its legal formalism, the central role played by language, culture, customs, and shared habits and values in terms of laying the foundations for a genuine 'recognition policy' impacting collective identities and rights.

1999; and Paul van Seters' *Communitarianism in Law and Society*, Rowman & Littlefield, Lanham, 2006.

In the eyes of communitarians, a pre-social notion of the 'I' is simply unthinkable, since every individual always encounters a pre-existing society — and it is thus the latter that determines his preferences, defines his worldly nature and shapes his aims. The fundamental idea is that the self is definitely *discovered* rather than *chosen*, because one cannot, by definition, choose what is already given. Self-understanding is therefore equivalent to gradually discovering what our nature and identity truly consist of. What follows from this is that one's socio-historical way of life is inseparable from one's identity, just as belonging to a community is inseparable from self-knowledge. Indeed, affiliations are part of the very identity of individuals, which not only implies that the latter exercise choice based on a given way of life (including choices that actually go against this lifestyle), but also that it is, once again, this modus vivendi which embodies, in terms of worth or worthlessness, what individuals consider to be acceptable or not.

A genuine community is thus not a mere gathering or amalgamation of individuals: indeed, owing to their very belonging, its members have common aspirations that relate to their shared values or experiences, and not only to some more or less congruent private interests. These aspirations are, likewise, specific to the community itself and not personal objectives that just so happen to be shared by all or most members. When merely part of associations, individuals regard their own interests as being independent and potentially divergent from one another's. The connections between these interests do not, therefore, represent anything good per se, but only serve as a means to attain whatever good is sought by each and every individual. A community, by contrast, embodies an intrinsic good from the perspective of all those who belong to it.

The liberal ideology has mostly interpreted the decline of the community phenomenon as closely related to the emergence of modernity — the more the modern world imposed itself as such, the more community ties were expected to slacken in favour of more voluntary and contractual means of association, of more individualistic and more rational behavioural patterns. Viewed from such an angle, communities came across as a residual phenomenon that institutional bureaucracies and global markets were destined to eradicate or dissolve. Ultimately, it is the prospect of a unified world that was supposed to take shape, not unlike Saint Augustine's 'heavenly city', which, according to him, 'calls citizens out of all nations, and gathers together a society of pilgrims of all languages, not scrupling about diversities in the manners, laws, and institutions'.[19]

This, however, was not to be. As written by Christopher Lasch,[20] 'uprootedness uproots everything except the need for roots!' The dissolution of the communities of old had previously been accelerated by the birth of the nation-state, an eminently *societal* phenomenon (with society defined as the loss or disintegration of communal intimacy) that one could readily connect, and not without reason, with the emergence of the individual as the supreme value.

Significantly, the crisis of the state-national model now goes hand in hand with the reappearance of political forms that reach beyond this model, both from the top (with the formation of continental blocks destined to play a key role in a multipolar world) and from the bottom (localist demands, the proliferation of 'communities' and 'tribes', the re-emergence of regional and transnational integration).

Establishing itself as one of the possible means of overcoming modernity, the community is simultaneously shaking off the 'archaic' status that sociology had long attributed to it. It thus comes across as a permanent form of human association rather than a mere 'stage' of history that the modern age is alleged to have abolished — a human association which, depending on the era, either loses or gains in importance to some extent. It can, of course, also take on new shapes.

---

19 AN: Saint Augustine, *City of God*, Book XIX, Chapter 17.

20 TN: A history professor at the University of Rochester, Robert Christopher Lasch (1 June 1932–14 February 1994) was also active as a historian, moralist and social critic.

Nowadays, it is not solely on the basis of their common origin that communities bring people together. Indeed, in a world where the various flows and networks are ever on the increase, communities come in a great diversity of forms, though it is always their very existence that allows individuals to stand no longer alone in the face of the state.

We are all familiar with the Maffesolian notion of post-modern 'tribes'. According to Michel Maffesoli,[21] post-modernity sanctions the end of the age of pure individualism, bringing with it a 'Dionysian' renaissance of the need for both local solidarity and community-related, palpable and emotional affiliations, as these communities can also be of the chosen — i.e. the 'elective and plural' — kind, being no less active than any other ones, even if they rarely manage to prove long-lasting. To Maffesoli, 'this anti-community enchantment only results in exacerbating the divide between the people and the elites': 'Beyond the narcissism or selfishness that characterises such predicated individualism, it is indeed a "we", namely that of the community and of shared vibrations, that tends to spread surreptitiously.'[22]

Distancing himself to some extent from Tönnies' approach, Costanzo Preve[23] believes, for his part, that it is society as a whole that must be transformed into a community. He thus writes:

> In no way is the capitalist society, especially when globalised, a community … A community is, in fact, a particular or universal type of human society, one that is not so much defined by the physical proximity of its members as by the presence of a certain set of customs (*ethos*), or of mores (*Sitten*), if you will — that is to say, by the existence of social ethics that prevail over any blind economic movements ruled by nihilism and relativism.[24]

---

21 TN: Born in 1944, Michel Maffesoli is a French sociologist.

22 AN: Michel Maffesoli and Hélène Strohl, *Les nouveaux bien-pensants* (The New Right-Minded Ones), Éditions du Moment, Paris, 2013, page 13.

23 TN: Costanzo Preve (14 April 1943–23 November 2013) was an Italian philosopher and political theoretician.

24 AN: Costanzo Preve, *Elogio del comunitarismo* (Praising Communitarianism), published in French as *Éloge du communautarisme*, Editions Krisis, Paris, 2012,

Costanzo Preve claims to be abiding by the ideas of Aristotle, Rousseau, Fichte, Hegel and Marx, all at the same time, stating that in the last case, class struggle itself is but a tactical means to achieve the strategic objective of a 'community' (*Gemeinwesen*) in which man would be able to find his natural generic being (*Gattungswesen*).[25] Preve is also careful to make a clear distinction between the communities that allow men to shape themselves and those that lock them into obsolete hierarchies. Denis Collin[26] expresses the very same opinion when saying that one must distinguish 'those communities that confine individuals to obeying patriarchal and despotic hierarchies from the community of free men'.[27]

Pointing out the 'absolutely central philosophical role that the first socialists bestowed upon the concepts of mutual aid and community', Jean-Claude Michéa[28] also promotes the 'criticism of the republican myth of the "universal", a myth of which the state is said to be the advocate, at least insofar as the "universal" is of the abstract kind and considered separate from, and contrary to, all that is particular and specific — meaning that grass-roots communities should, in short, renounce everything that sets them apart in order to merge into the great uniform family of the nation or the human race. Ever faithful to Hegelian principles, [it] espouses the belief that, by contrast, a specific universal is always a result (a temporary one, by definition) that comprises particularity as part of an essential phase, that is to say not as a "lesser evil", but as a sine qua non condition of its real effectiveness.'[29]

---

page 213.

25 AN: Ibid., page 32.

26 TN: A French philosopher.

27 AN: Denis Collin, 'La forme achevée de la République est la République sociale' (The Finished Form of the Republic Is a Social Republic), published in *Le Comptoir* [an electronic journal] on 3 November 2014, page 4.

28 TN: Jean-Claude Michéa is a retired philosophy professor, philosopher and writer.

29 AN: 'On ne peut être politiquement orthodoxe' (One Cannot Be Politically Orthodox), online text, January 2015.

Such is the eternal dialectic of the one and the manifold, of the universal and the individual.

A professor at the University of Ottawa, Stéphane Vibert remarks:

> The Left's diversity-preaching and progressive ideology are in perfect harmony with the individualistic liberalism advocated by the Right, since they both deny the historical and essential framework that gives specific meaning to the rights and duties of every citizen. Believing that society is based on a contract concluded by rational, free and moral individuals, or that it is shaped by automatic regulatory mechanisms stemming from the market, are two identical versions of the same liberal myth. This double fiction results in an *ersatz* political community that is incapable of understanding its own history and cultural foundations … It is time neo-republicans realised that a political community cannot be solely founded on principles of co-existence, as it is also — and above all — rooted in historical tradition defined as a permanent re-interpretation of all that binds us.[30]

---

30 AN: Stéphane Vibert, 'L'égalité dans la différence est un slogan creux' (Equality in Difference Is a Hollow Slogan), published in *Causeur*, October 2013, page 48.

L'INSTITUT ILIADE FOR LONG EUROPEAN MEMORY

L'Institut Iliade for Long European Memory, based in France, was born from an observation. Europe is but a shadow of her former self. Replaced by outsiders, confused by having lost their bearing and their pride, Europeans have abandoned the reins of their common destiny to people other than themselves. Europeans no longer remember. Why? Because amongst the current elite — whether at school, university, or in the media — no one passes down to them the cultural wealth of which they are the inheritors.

Contrary to this moribund current, L'Institut Iliade has given itself the task of participating in the renewal of the cultural grandeur of Europe and in aiding Europeans' reappropriation of their own identity. Facing the Great Erasure of culture, we intend to work for the Great Awakening of European consciousness and to help prepare Europe for a new renaissance — one of identity, freedom, and power.

L'Institut Iliade's calling is threefold:

- To train young men and young women concerned about their history to always build. To make them the avantgarde of the renaissance for which the Institut calls: men and women capable of giving to civic and political action that cultural and metapolitical dimension which is indispensable. Their motto: to put themselves at the service of a community of destiny, which risks disappearing if it is not taken in hand. Armed with a strong culture relating to European traditions and values, they learn to discern that the adventure that awaits them entails risks and self-sacrifice, but also enthusiasm and joy.

• To promote a radical and alternative vision of the world contrary to the dogmas of universalism, egalitarianism, and 'diversity'. Using all available means, the Institut develops concepts and ammunition to understand and fight the modern world.

• To gather together, especially — but not only — in France, those who refuse to submit and who are inspired daily by the Homeric triad as described by Dominique Venner: nature as the base, excellence as the goal, beauty as the horizon.

L'Institut Iliade's originality, especially with the aim of reformulating and updating knowledge, lies in tying together the seriousness of its content with ease of learning for the greater public, the objective being to demonstrate an authentic pedagogy, and to act in complementary or supportive ways with other initiatives having the same goal.

L'Institut Iliade's action takes place across various channels:

• A cadre school of the European Rebirth, which every year brings together trainees from a wide variety of backgrounds and is already seeing citizens from other European countries participate;

• an annual colloquium — made up of academics, politicians, writers, journalists, and association officials from all over Europe — that meets in Paris to discuss strong and challenging themes, such as 'The Aesthetic Universe of Europeans', 'Facing the Migratory Assault', 'Transmit or Disappear', 'Nature as Base — for an Ecology of Place', 'Beyond the Market — Economy at the Service of Peoples';

- the publication of works—designed as beacons to enlighten readers' thoughts and guide them toward the reconquest of their identity—within several collections, made available in the widest array of languages and European countries;

- artistic exhibitions on the fringes of contemporary artistic trends, allowing the public to take a fresh look at art and rooted creation;

- an incubator for ideas, businesses, and associations to support and help the greatest number of projects—with quality and sustainability criteria—across all fields of civil society (culture, commerce, etc.) that seek to impose a rooted vision of the world and an alternative to the current system, while prioritising structures and projects making an impact in real life;

- an active presence on social media, allowing us to reach new audiences (through videos, publications, annual events, and news presentations), centred around a website that functions as much as a resource hub as it does as a platform for exchanges and debate, notably offering an ideal library of more than five hundred works, a European primer, a dictionary of quotations, and turnkey itineraries for visiting and hiking the prominent places of European memory.

Education through history:

L'Institut Iliade endeavours to uphold in every circumstance the richness and singularity of our heritage in order to draw forth the source and the resources of a serene, but determined, affirmation of our identity, both national and European. In line with the thought and deeds of Dominique Venner, the Institut accords in all its activities an essential place to history, both as a matrix of deep meditation on the future as well as a place of the unexpected, where anything is possible.

CONCERNING EUROPE, it seems as though we will be forced to rise up and face immense challenges and fearsome catastrophes even beyond those posed by immigration. These hardships will present the opportunity for both a rebirth and a rediscovery of ourselves. I believe in those qualities that are specific to the European people, qualities currently in a state of dormancy. I believe in our active individuality, our inventiveness, and in the awakening of our energy. This awakening will undoubtedly come. When? I do not know, but I am positive that it will take place.

— DOMINIQUE VENNER, *The Shock of History*
Arktos Media, London, 2015

Follow L'Institut Iliade at
www.institut-iliade.com
linktr.ee/InstitutILIADE

OTHER BOOKS PUBLISHED BY ARKTOS

OTHER BOOKS PUBLISHED BY ARKTOS

OTHER BOOKS PUBLISHED BY ARKTOS

www.ingramcontent.com/pod-product-compliance
Lightning Source LLC
Chambersburg PA
CBHW032122280326
41933CB00009B/950